D0369119

JOHN 8:12

PSALM 34:8

PROJECT TITLE:

Blueprints for Life
Building on the Foundation of Christ

ARCHITECT: JESUS CHRIST

REV. 3:20

GENESIS 28:1_

DEUTERONOMY 6:4-9

JOHN 1:4-5

1 PETER 1:6-8

Tim Wesemann

www.CTAinc.com

Blueprints for Life
Building on the Foundation of Christ
by Tim Wesemann

www.timwesemann.com

Birdhouse blueprints provided by Steve Matlock
of the Matlock Group, St. Louis, MO.

About the cover Scripture references:

Isaiah 33:6 and Matthew 16:18 remind us of the sure foundation of our lives. The
true church is built on the profession that Jesus is the Christ, the Son of the Living God.

Deuteronomy 6:4–9 teaches us that God's ways should joyfully be taught in every room
of our homes.

Psalm 34:8 brings us into a divine kitchen where we taste and see the goodness of our Lord.

Genesis 28:12–15 recalls Jacob's dream of the heavenly stairway, reminding us of God's
promises and presence.

John 1:4–5 and 8:12 evoke thoughts of *the* Light, which gracefully shines in our homes.

Combining the hearth with 1 Peter 1:6–8, we remember the fire of trials that refines our faith.

The words of Revelation 3:20 knock on the door of our hearts, and we welcome
Christ into our hearts and lives through the power of the Holy Spirit.

ISBN 1-933234-15-6
Printed in Thailand

To: _____

*[God] decided from the outset
to shape the lives of those
who love him along the same lines
as the life of his Son.*

Romans 8:29 THE MESSAGE

Join me in
celebrating his plans
for your life!

From: _____

Date: _____

BIRDHOUSE

As you come to him, a living stone rejected by men but in the sight of God chosen and precious, you yourselves like living stones are being built up as a spiritual house, to be a holy priesthood, to offer spiritual sacrifices acceptable to God through Jesus Christ. For it stands in Scripture:
"Behold, I am laying in Zion a stone, a cornerstone chosen and precious, and whoever believes in him will not be put to shame."

1 Peter 2:4–6

For no one can lay any other foundation than the one we already have—Jesus Christ.

1 Corinthians 3:11 NLT

Table of Contents

Christ is our cornerstone,
On him alone we build;
With his true saints alone
The courts of heav'n are filled.
On his great love our hopes we place
Of present grace and joys above.

Author unknown, Latin, 700
tr. John Chandler, 1806–76

[Jesus said:]
"Everyone then who
hears these words
of mine and does them
will be like a wise man
who built his house
on the rock.
And the rain fell,
and the floods came,
and the winds blew
and beat on that house,
but it did not fall,
because it had been
founded on the rock.
And everyone who hears
these words of mine and
does not do them will be
like a foolish man
who built his house
on the sand.
And the rain fell,
and the floods came,
and the winds blew
and beat against that
house, and it fell,
and great was the fall
of it."

Matthew 7:24-27

Getting Started

This is for the birds!

N o. Let me reword that. Some of this book is for the birds. The majority includes encouragement, direction, and inspiration. In these pages we will explore room by room, from foundation to roof, the house called life, which God has designed masterfully, individually, specially, for each of us.

But wait, there's more!

(No, this isn't an infomercial, even though that line sounded like one!) As each chapter begins, you will find the next step in a set of instructions for building a simple but functional birdhouse. (I told you some of this book is for the birds!)

God will use the message of this book to help you grow in your relationship with him. As he does that, the birdhouse project can serve as a way that you can strengthen a relationship you enjoy with another person in your life.

Would a child, a neighbor, or a relative enjoy spending time with you? You can build the birdhouse together as a way of helping your relationship with that person grow. And even if you build the birdhouse by yourself instead, you'll be taking part in God's plan and promise to care for his creation.

> *Look at the birds of the air; they do not sow or reap or store away in barns, and yet your heavenly Father feeds them. Are you not much more valuable than they?*
>
> Matthew 6:26 NIV

Birds of the air!

Blueprints for Living

God has a marvelous design in mind for your life. Do you believe that? I hope so. It's true! Your Creator has laid out a blueprint over your life. The Architect's lines have fallen across your life in the shape of the life of his Son, your Savior, Jesus Christ.

Maybe a visual will help communicate this. Do you remember the grade-school project in which your teacher cut a long piece of paper from a roll of paper, and you lay on it while someone traced around your body to create an outline?

Once you had the outline, you turned it into a life-sized portrait, a living you, one with face, features, flaws, and all.

Similarly, the outline that God has drawn around and over our lives traces the perfect life of his Son—our Savior, Christ Jesus. We live with Christ and in Christ:

> *I have been crucified with Christ and I no longer live, but Christ lives in me. The life I live in the body, I live by faith in the Son of God, who loved me and gave himself for me.*
>
> Galatians 2:20

Does this mean we live exempt from the hurts, troubles, illnesses, and death that come from living in a sinful world? No, it doesn't. But we do have God's promise to walk with us, to give us hope, and to work continually for the good of all who love him, in good times and in troubling circumstances alike.

A Designer's Life

Whether we realize it or not, we live a designer life. The only question centers on who does the designing. Is yours a life built by your own designs or by divine design?

Living "by faith in the Son of God" (Galatians 2:20) means we live by God's design. We live a life possible only because the forgiveness, wisdom, and strength of our God work abundant life within us. We respond to his undeserved love for us in Jesus by loving him and others. It's all in the blueprints.

You may be familiar with Ephesians 2:8–9. You may even have committed it to memory:

> *For it is by grace you have been saved, through faith—and this not from yourselves, it is the gift of God—not by works, so that no one can boast.*

NIV

But what about the next verse? As we consider God's design for our lives, we need to look at it, too:

> *For we are God's workmanship, created in Christ Jesus to do good works, which God prepared in advance for us to do.*

Ephesians 2:10 NIV

My Life—A God-Story

Grace, salvation, faith, *and* good works—it's *all* part of the God-story written across our lives. We can't take any of the credit for the design itself, but we can find joy in living by God's design, in carrying out those acts of love he has prepared in advance for us to do.

With that in mind, and as God works by his Holy Spirit in our hearts, this book intends to

- help you build upon your sure foundation, Jesus Christ;
- encourage you in your faith walk;
- inspire you to respond in joy and power to God's blueprints for an abundant life;
- motivate you to new avenues of service;
- strengthen you when you need rest;
- help you proclaim the riches of God's grace;
- support you in your relationships (especially if you select to build the birdhouse with someone); and
- give your God—the Architect of creation and salvation—all the glory and praise he deserves!

As you study the blueprints for true life that Christ sets before you, may the Spirit of God continue to build you up in your faith and may you find great joy in living by God's design to the glory of his name!

So this is what the Sovereign
LORD says:
"See, I lay a stone in Zion,
a tested stone,
a precious cornerstone
for a sure foundation;
the one who trusts
will never be dismayed.

Isaiah 28:16 NIV

He will be the sure foundation
for your times,
a rich store of salvation
and wisdom and knowledge;
the fear of the LORD
is the key to this treasure.

Isaiah 33:6 NIV

This is for us . . .

The Foundation

Without a solid foundation, any building will eventually collapse. Our lives work that way, too. Those who live by God's design rest fully on the only secure foundation—Jesus Christ, his death and resurrection.

Many prophets of the Old Testament wrote about this:

> *I love you, O LORD, my strength. The LORD is my rock and my fortress and my deliverer, my God, my rock, in whom I take refuge, my shield, and the horn of my salvation, my stronghold. I call upon the LORD, who is worthy to be praised, and I am saved from my enemies.*
>
> Psalm 18:1–3

> *Hear my cry, O God, listen to my prayer; from the end of the earth I call to you when my heart is faint. Lead me to the rock that is higher than I.*
>
> Psalm 61:1–2

> *Righteousness and justice are the foundation of your throne; steadfast love and faithfulness go before you.*
>
> Psalm 89:14

> *But the LORD has become my stronghold, and my God the rock of my refuge.*
>
> Psalm 94:22

Rock-Solid

Jesus is our stronghold, our fortress, the secure, immovable footing on which God's faithful live. He described himself in these terms as he wrapped up the teaching that has come to be known as the Sermon on the Mount (Matthew 5–7). He said:

> *These words I speak to you*
> *are not incidental additions to your life,*
> *homeowner improvements*
> *to your standard of living.*
> *They are foundational words,*
> *words to build a life on.*
>
> *If you work these words into your life,*
> *you are like a smart carpenter*
> *who built his house on solid rock.*
> *Rain poured down, the river flooded,*
> *a tornado hit—*
> *but nothing moved that house.*
> *It was fixed to the rock.*
>
> *But if you just use my words in Bible studies*
> *and don't work them into your life,*
> *you are like a stupid carpenter*
> *who built his house on the sandy beach.*
> *When a storm rolled in and the waves came up,*
> *it collapsed like a house of cards.*

Matthew 7:24–27 THE MESSAGE

> Jesus is our stronghold, our fortress, the secure, immovable footing on which God's faithful live.

These are powerful words, words on which to build a life. But if we're honest with ourselves, we can become quite disheartened as we read Jesus' words, recognizing just how far short we fall in living out God's design for our lives.

How thankful we can be, though, in knowing that Christ is our foundation for life now and life forever. Built upon him as our foundation, we find grace and forgiveness in his cross when we fail. Our God is a God of second (and third and fourth) chances, a God of unending new opportunities.

Fortress

Sandy Alternatives

O ur lives rest on the immovable foundation of grace and forgiveness in Jesus Christ. Still, we sometimes find ourselves wandering about, looking for something more.

Satan tempts us to play in his ballpark. He somehow manages to make his sandy field of poisonous weeds look like greener grass. Friends whose lives rest on sand instead of on Christ also urge us to play on their team. If we listen, we can soon find ourselves sitting on the bench in Satan's sandy field of deceit while the world goes to bat for us. Our own sinful nature can rear its ugly head, too, and before we know it, we begin to play the world's favorite game: "I Know Better than God."

Scripture records a world-class round of that game played on a construction site called Babel. I toured that site once, and I remember my trip there like it was yesterday. My Sunday school teacher, Mrs. Lohr, booked the tour through the Flannelgraph Travel Agency when I was in her class. What an amazing trip!

As the story from Genesis 11 unfolded through those flannel figures, my classmates and I learned that wicked people gathered in Babel to build a city. Their plan for that city included a tower that would "reach to the heavens." By building the world's first skyscraper, they would "make a name for [themselves]" (verse 4).

But their building committee made two major mistakes:

- First, they forgot to consult the Architect—the one who designed and created a once-flawless world.
- Second, they set out to build their city by themselves, for themselves. They wanted the glory, the power, and the name for themselves. Honoring the Lord could not have been further from their thoughts.

By making these two errors, they built their city and tower on a foundation of sand, as it were. But even though God's people forgot him, he did not forget them.

For their own good, God intervened in the people's selfish, sinful, foolish plans. He "came down" to their puny construction site and made one simple change in plans, confusing their language so the builders could no longer understand each other. Construction at Babel came to a halt.

Sand

Satan's Schemes

Babel shows us that only what the Lord builds will stand eternally. Today he is at work in the lives of his believers, actively constructing those lives upon the sure foundation of Jesus Christ.

However, just as Satan long ago watched God's process, looking desperately for ways to stop it, so he watches and schemes today, desperate to halt God's process.

Satan skillfully manipulates his tools. He hammers bitterness into our hearts. He leaves vices lying around to tempt us. He tries to saw our solid relationships into pieces. He uses a fake level to give the false impression of healthy balance in our lives. He whittles down our relationships with his tools of jealousy, out-of-control anger, spite, and a desire for vengeance. He nails us with words from others that hurt.

> Knowing Jesus, we can build a life of true joy.

Still, we can rest on our foundation and cornerstone, Jesus Christ. The plans developed by the Architect and Contractor of our faith can withstand the schemes of Satan. Jesus clearly communicated this to us without words from another construction site—actually a *reconstruction site.* There, Roman nails pinned our Savior to a wooden cross. Wordlessly, that act communicated his commitment to us and his love for us.

From that construction site still today, Jesus builds bridges between human beings and a holy God by forgiving sin. From there, he renews hope for reconciliation between human beings estranged from each other, too.

Knowing Jesus, we can build a life of true joy. He is the foundation, the only foundation for true and everlasting life in relationship with our God.

Thinking about Foundations

F ew people spend a lot of time thinking about the foundation on which their home is built. I've only considered my own home's foundation twice: during the building engineer's inspection before my wife and I bought the house, and at a time when we had some flooding in our area and water seeped in through the foundation.

In reality, I live each day on a foundation I take for granted. Being able to trust my home's foundation and forget about it is a good thing.

But as God's people we do not want to ignore our spiritual foundation. We want to think often and deeply about how much Jesus means to us. We want to overflow with praise and thanksgiving in response.

When the rain pours down and the rivers rise, we hope the foundation of our earthly house will stand firm. We don't want the sill plates, tie bolts, pilasters, piers, rebars, and pads that make up the foundations of our earthly home or apartment building to fail.

But no matter what happens to our house here on earth, we can know that our spiritual foundation in Christ stands eternal. The salvation, love, forgiveness, peace, comfort, faithfulness, joy, and grace that make up that foundation will never fail us. They are immovable.

Jesus is the solid rock of our salvation. He is the high place of safety on which we stand. Not even the strictest building inspector in the world will find defects in that foundation.

We may not pay much attention to the foundation on which our physical home or apartment building rests, but we'd be foolish to ignore the foundation on which our faith and lives have been built—Jesus Christ! What a difference that security makes!

> *Therefore, as you received Christ Jesus the Lord, so walk in him, rooted and built up in him and established in the faith, just as you were taught, abounding in thanksgiving.*

Colossians 2:6–7

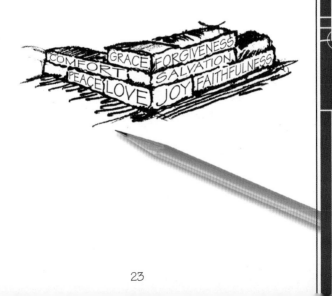

Hear, O Israel:
The LORD our God,
the LORD is one.
You shall love the LORD your
God with all your heart
and with all your soul and
with all your might.
And these words that I
command you today
shall be on your heart.
You shall teach them
diligently to your children,
and shall talk of them when
you sit in your house, and
when you walk by the way,
and when you lie down,
and when you rise.
You shall bind them as a sign
on your hand,
and they shall be as frontlets
between your eyes.
You shall write them on the
doorposts of your house
and on your gates.

Deuteronomy 6:4-9

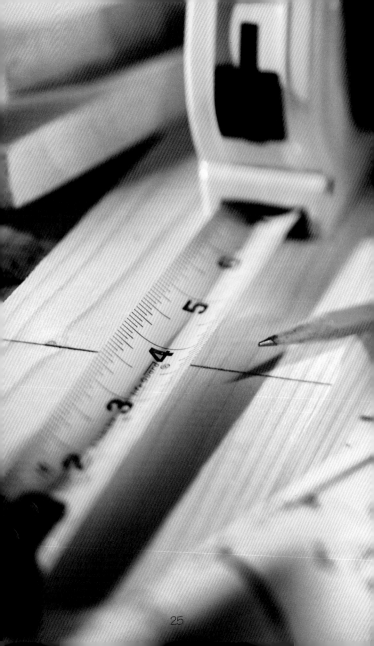

This is for the birds . . .

Traditional Birdhouse Design

Materials:

1 ea.	1" x 6" x 6'-0" Rough sawn cedar board
1 ea.	3/8" dia. x 6" long wood dowel
30	4d finish nails
1 tube	Exterior wood adhesive

Tools Required:

Wood Saw
Finish Hammer
Power Drill
1 1/2" Paddle Bit
3/8" Dia. Wood Drill Bit
Caulking Gun (for glue)

STEP #1

Cut two (2) side wall panels as indicated in figures "a1" & "a2"

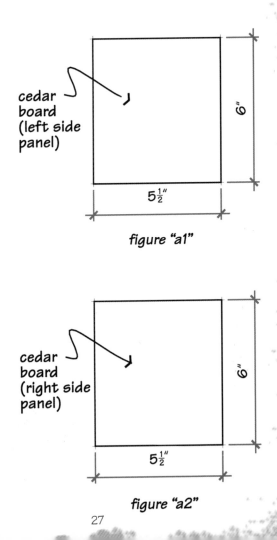

cedar board (left side panel)

6"

5½"

figure "a1"

cedar board (right side panel)

6"

5½"

figure "a2"

This is for us . . .

The Family Room

I'm not sure the term *family room* means the same thing it did some years ago. When family rooms first appeared on blueprints, families used them as less formal, more casual rooms in which to do things together as a family. When constructed, family rooms often housed a toy chest, a cabinet stocked with board games, a card table covered with a jigsaw puzzle, a bookcase loaded with books, a sound system, comfortable seating, and usually the family television set—the only family television set.

Today fewer people have a family room. At least, fewer new homes call them that. How about your home, your family?

- Do you spend time playing board games together? Or is your family bored with games?
- Would your family look puzzled if you'd suggest putting a puzzle together?
- Have you booked any time for reading books lately? (Please pity this author and tell me some families do still read!)
- I'm sure you watch television. But do you watch TV together, or does everyone have his or her own set to watch in an individual corner of the house?

I'm not trying to guilt you into considering lifestyle changes. But as you consider with me ways to live more consistently with God's design, I do hope to give you cause for reflection. In some cases, this might instigate repentance and therefore lead to some lifestyle modifications. I certainly know my own family could use some changing. We're all in this together!

> Our heart's desire is to beat in unison with God's own heartbeat.

Living on the foundation of Jesus Christ and in God's family, our heart's desire is to beat in unison with God's own heartbeat. What does he want for our family? Having a family room or not makes little difference. But our Lord does want us to make room in our lives for our family members. He wants our concern for their faith walk to take a prominent place on our list of high-priority issues. He cares that we worship together weekly at his holy altar rather than at the unholy one that comes with a remote control and 150 channels.

150 Channels!

My Shepherd?

M aybe you've seen this takeoff on Psalm 23. I'd like to give credit to its author, but in every version I have found, the author is unknown:

The TV is my shepherd; I shall not want.
*   It maketh me to lie down on the sofa.*
*   It leadeth me away from the Scriptures.*
*   It destroyeth my soul.*
*   It leadeth me in the paths of immorality,*
*   for the sponsor's sake.*
Yea, though I walk in the shadow of my
*   responsibilities,*
*   there will be no interruptions,*
*   for the TV is with me.*
*   Its cable and wireless controls, they comfort me.*
*   It prepareth a commercial before me,*
*   in the presence of my carnality.*
*   It anointeth my head with humanism.*
*   My coveting runneth over.*
Surely laziness and ignorance shall follow me all the
*   days of my life,*
*   and I shall dwell in the family room*
*   with my TV forever.*

While the parody rings true, certainly the inventor of the television can't take all the blame! What or who is the *family altar* in your home?

The "family room" holds special prominence in the blueprint God has designed for the lives of his people. While he does create special designs that call some to live single lives, he has also said that it is not good to be alone. For this reason he brings men and women together in family units (Genesis 2:18), telling us to be fruitful and multiply, bringing children into our families (Genesis 1:28).

Can you imagine an absolutely perfect marriage or family? That's how God first constructed the family—on a perfect foundation. His perfection has not changed, even though we, his human creations, have. What a long, long way from perfection we have come! We've moved in exactly the wrong direction!

We've done the equivalent of spilling coffee all over God's designs for our lives, our households. As I consider the reality of my sin, I'm overwhelmed with gratitude that Jesus makes every stain disappear. His blood poured out on the blueprints doesn't make a mess; rather it shouts out his "Yes!"

> *"Yes! I forgive you."*
> *"Yes! I love you."*
> *"Yes! I accept you."*
> *"Yes! You're part of my family."*
> *"Yes! No matter the mess you make,*
> *I will help you clean it up!"*

Marriage

God's Yes

God's "Yes!" makes it possible to call our family together . . .

- to spend more time with each other;
- to care about each other's faith;
- to play together and pray together;
- to laugh together and cry together;
- to plan together;
- to talk to each other and listen to each other;
- to forgive as we have been forgiven;
- to learn together;
- to love each other; and
- to worship together at the altar of the one and only God—Father, Son, and Holy Spirit—who calls us to be part of his family.

Give Thanks!

God moves in to straighten up our "family room." His plans include more than simply moving the furniture around a bit; he plans to completely redecorate, to update and to upgrade our family's whole look, a look that reflects his joy and peace!

Because he continually forgives and continually rearranges our lives, we can offer up prayers of praise and thanksgiving to him. Psalm 136 provides a model for us as we celebrate God's forever, foundational love for us. It reminds us of his grace. It encourages us as we face the future. In the original psalm, one phrase repeats twenty-six times: *His love endures forever.*

The psalmist uses this phrase to thank the Lord as he reviews the history of his people from the Garden of Eden to the time they entered the Promised Land. I encourage you to take time to read the psalm in its entirety.

Here is a contemporary family psalm based on the praise and prayers of Psalm 136. Maybe you'll want to read it with a family member:

Give thanks to the Lord, for he is good!
> *His love endures forever!*
He knew us before we were a family;
> *his love endures forever!*
He created the world and our faith
> through his Word;
> *his love endures forever!*
He allowed our children to take their
> first steps and gave them the Spirit-created
> ability to follow in his steps;
> *his love endures forever!*
He gives us shelter and food while sheltering us
> with his love as we drink from his living water;
> *his love endures forever!*
He carried us through weeks of chicken pox
> and healed all our diseases;
> *his love endures forever!*
He led us with compassion through times of darkness
> and family deaths directly into the promises
> of eternal life;
> *his love endures forever!*
To him who entrusts us with more than we need and more
> than we ask for—
> *his love endures forever!*

We walk with confidence and joy as a family
    within his family, knowing
        his love endures forever!
He gave the life of his only Son up on the cross
    for this family and all families, for
        his love endures forever!
Give thanks to the Lord, for he is good!
        His love endures forever!

Are you ready to call a family meeting in the family room?
(Don't forget to invite your Father!)

His love endures forever!

Why is everyone hungry for
more? "More, more," they say.
"More, more." I have God's
more-than-enough,
More joy in one ordinary day
Than they get in all their
shopping sprees.

Psalm 4:6–7 THE MESSAGE

You're blessed when you've
worked up a good appetite for
God. He's food and drink in the
best meal you'll ever eat.

Matthew 5:6 THE MESSAGE

Oh, taste and see
that the LORD is good!
Blessed is the man
who takes refuge in him!

Psalm 34:8

The spirit of God whets our
appetite by giving us a taste
of what's ahead. He puts a little
of heaven in our hearts
so that we'll never
settle for less.

2 Corinthians 5:5 THE MESSAGE

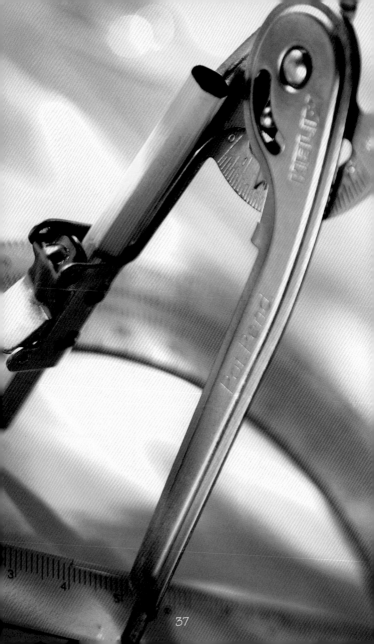

This is for the birds . . .

STEP #2

Cut out front wall panel as
indicated in figure "b"

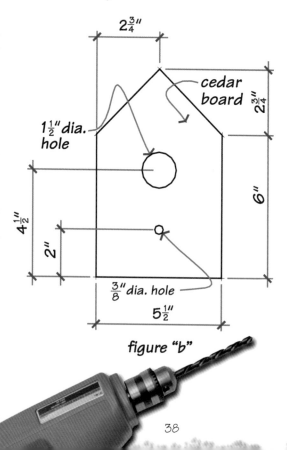

$2\frac{3}{4}''$

cedar
board

$2\frac{3}{4}''$

$1\frac{1}{2}''$ dia.
hole

$4\frac{1}{2}''$

$2''$

6"

$\frac{3}{8}''$ dia. hole

$5\frac{1}{2}''$

figure "b"

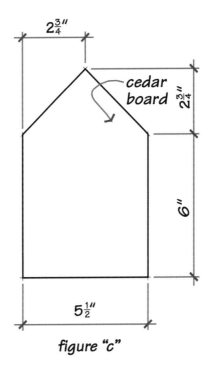

$2\frac{3}{4}''$

cedar board

$2\frac{3}{4}''$

$6''$

$5\frac{1}{2}''$

figure "c"

STEP #3

Cut out rear wall panel as indicated in figure "c". Use front wall panel (fig. "b") as a template for the rear panel to ensure both panels are identical.

This is for us . . .

The Kitchen

My eyes quickly scan the blueprints. How many feet from the front door? Just down the hall from the family room, right? Ahh, there it is—the kitchen! I can hardly wait to explore it! You see, I have a problem (one of many). It's a *wait* problem. I can't *wait* for the next meal! So I snack and snack and snack and now . . . I have a *weight* problem!

One day while waiting for my microwavable chocolate-flavored macaroni and cheese to cook, I realized I wasn't the only one with a *wait* problem. This verse printed on a recipe card and taped to a cupboard door caught my eye:

I wait for the LORD, my soul waits, and in his word I hope; my soul waits for the Lord more than watchmen for the morning, more than watchmen for the morning. O, Israel, hope in the LORD! For with the LORD there is steadfast love, And with him is plentiful redemption.

Psalm 130:5–7

Plentiful redemption. Now that's something I could sink my teeth into. And it was right in front of me. Right there in the kitchen. I checked the nutritional value and found only nutrients to nourish my faith.

Taste and See

The Lord's plentiful redemption . . .

- healthier than the freshest salad;
- better tasting than sweet corn on the cob plucked from the stalk just a few hours before cooking;
- juicier than a tenderloin steak perfectly prepared;
- more filling than Mom's mashed potatoes;
- sweeter and richer than a just-out-of-the-oven chocolate-chip cookie; and
- more satisfying than a cold glass of water on a hot and humid summer day.

Can't you almost taste it? What wonderful aroma! Just talking about it makes the cravings start. Wait! I'll be right back!

Okay, I've returned. Please forgive my absence, but I couldn't wait any longer. God's plentiful redemption is every bit as satisfying as I described. I don't mind admitting I ran to the kitchen for a taste. No, not the kitchen in my house, but rather the one marked out on God's blueprints for my life and yours.

I found this on the right front burner:

> [The Lord says,] "I, even I, am he who blots out your transgressions, for my own sake, and remembers your sins no more."
>
> Isaiah 43:25 NIV

This sat on the left front burner:

*Peace I leave with you; my peace I give to you.
Not as the world gives do I give to you. Let not your
hearts be troubled, neither let them be afraid.*

John 14:27

I discovered this in the pantry:

*The eyes of all look to you, and you give them their
food in due season.*

Psalm 145:15

And these goodies sat nearby on a plate:

*Keep yourselves in God's love as you wait for the mercy
of our Lord Jesus Christ to bring you to eternal life.*

Jude 21 NIV

*To him who is able to keep you from falling and to
present you before his glorious presence without fault
and with great joy—to the only God our Savior be
glory, majesty, power and authority, through Jesus
Christ our Lord, before all ages, now and forevermore!
Amen.*

Jude 24–25 NIV

Filling and Nourishing

Talk about satisfying! And it's only a snack. There's so much more in the kitchen! Check it out for yourself. If you crave something God-pleasing, you'll be sure to find it on the menu.

> *You've had a taste of God. Now, like infants at the breast, drink deep of God's pure kindness. Then you'll grow up mature and whole in God.*
>
> 1 Peter 2:3; 2:2 THE MESSAGE

Our Lord wants us to become connoisseurs of his grace, savoring every morsel and sip of what he serves up for our soul's nourishment and healing. Our Father delights in serving us, his children, and he supplies every need of ours according to his riches in the glory in Christ Jesus (Philippians 4:19).

Not only does God supply all our needs, he even takes care of those little touches that make kitchens places to warm the heart. Take, for instance, the note that hangs on the refrigerator under a cross-shaped magnet, a note written by our Father:

> *I love being the Giver of heavenly flavors.*
>
> *I want you to learn the art of the connoisseur!*

Like Ezekiel, learn to appreciate my Word—sweet as honey.

Take and drink my pure, life-giving milk: my kindness in Christ!

You will grow strong in faith as you feast on my food, having tasted that I am good.

Based on Ezekiel 3:3; 1 Peter 2:2–3; and Psalm 34:8–10

Spiritually hungry? Dying of thirst? You'll find God's heavenly kitchen open 24/7! His never-ending buffet serves all who come to eat of the Bread of Life and drink of the Living Water, Jesus Christ. God reserves a place at his table for you! And there's no charge—it's all on the house, God's house of grace.

So, what are you waiting for?

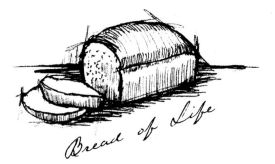

Bread of Life

Rock of Ages, cleft for me,
Let me hide myself in thee;
Let the water and the blood,
From thy riven side
which flowed,
Be of sin the double cure:
Cleanse me from its guilt
and pow'r.

Augustus M. Toplady, 1740–78

How can a young man keep his way pure? By guarding it according to your word. With my whole heart I seek you; let me not wander from your commandments! I have stored up your word in my heart, that I might not sin against you. Blessed are you, O Lord; Teach me your statutes! With my lips I declare all the rules of your mouth. In the way of your testimonies I delight as much as in all riches. I will meditate on your precepts and fix my eyes on your ways. I will delight in your statutes; I will not forget your word.

Psalm 119:9–16

196

EN.

This is for the birds . . .

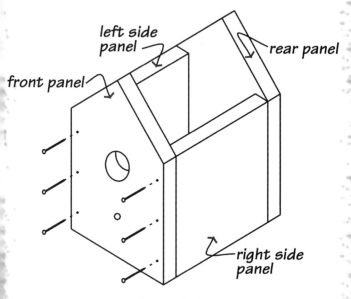

left side panel

rear panel

front panel

right side panel

figure "d"

STEP #4

Assemble front, rear and side panels as shown in fig. "d". Glue and nail (3 nails per joint as indicated) each joint.

48

STEP #5

Cut out bottom panel by placing assembled walls (fig. "d") over cedar board. Mark edges to be cut by tracing the inside of birdhouse walls as indicated in figure "e". Cut on traced line. Install bottom panel inside assembled walls with adhesive and nails (2 nails per side).

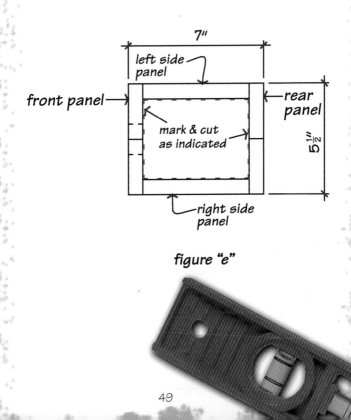

figure "e"

This is for us . . .

The Study

ouses in the past sometimes included a study. It tended to be decorated as though that room belonged to the man of the house. The tradition may go back as far as the days of Ward Cleaver (not the reruns—the first run!). But even though the male dominance of the study probably vanished after the networks cancelled *Leave It to Beaver*, I know God included a study in his blueprints for the lives of the men of God—your life and mine. In fact, I think the study is an essential part of a life built on the foundation of Christ, a life lived by God's divine design.

A study is for studying, right? We certainly have a God who can teach us a thing or two! But how much studying do we do, really? And what do we study?

(Do you homeschool your children? Once I needed to converse with a homeschooling parent. But as I approached him, I noticed he was talking to himself. Fearing I might interrupt a parent-teacher consultation, I thought it best to keep on walking!)

Later?

nfortunately, when it comes to studying the blueprint for living that God reveals in his Word, too many of us put it off until later. We walk past opportunities. Listen to the words of someone who made wise use of the study in his home built on the sure foundation:

> *I'm asking God for one thing, only one thing:*
> *To live with him in his house my whole life long.*
> *I'll contemplate his beauty; I'll study at his feet.*
>
> Psalm 27:4 THE MESSAGE

Yes, that's the study God designed for us! Our Lord decorated the study with "Psalm 27:4 wallpaper"! The mantle and desk come engraved with these words. The passage scrolls across the computer screensaver.

Of course, we expect to find one book in this room—*the* Book. The Bible. After all, it is the true, inspired Word of God, the account of his love for us and what that love led him to do for us in our Savior, Jesus.

But the Lord also blesses us with extrabiblical resources: books, CDs, DVDs, devotionals, Bible studies, commentaries, computer-reference programs, and more—enough to fill every shelf in the study! We need to choose these with discernment. As the apostle John cautions us in these inspired words:

> *Beloved, do not believe every spirit, but test the spirits to see whether they are from God, for many false prophets have gone out into the world.*
>
> 1 John 4:1

Library

Power to Touch Hands, Hearts

And as we hold on to the Word of God, we must also respect the power of that Word in our hands and our hearts. The words of Law will pierce our hearts, convicting us of our sin and our desperate need for a Savior:

For the word of God is living and active, sharper than any two-edged sword, piercing to the division of soul and of spirit, of joints and of marrow, and discerning the thoughts and intentions of the heart. And no creature is hidden from his sight, but all are naked and exposed to the eyes of him to whom we must give account.

Hebrews 4:12–13

If we think we can hide away in a study from God's scrutiny, we're mistaken. But wait! That's not the only focus of the study! While the Law of God is powerful enough to show our sins and need for a Savior, the Good News of our Savior and his cross, also found in Scripture, brings us hope, forgiveness, and eternal life.

Yes, sin pays its wages—death. But . . . the gift of God is eternal life in Jesus Christ, our Lord (Romans 6:23)!

We cannot emphasize the importance of a study—our study of all of God's Word—nearly enough. That Word guides our daily walk with the Savior, as it also impacts those around us. But we can't stay in the study! We live in the world outside the study.

No matter where we go in life, people around us constantly observe how we respond to situations. What we say, how we live, how we treat others—all we do falls under scrutiny. We come out of the study to carry the message of Christ's love to others. Scripture puts it this way:

You are a letter from Christ delivered by us, written not with ink but with the Spirit of the living God, not on tablets of stone but on tablets of human hearts.

2 Corinthians 3:3

What a responsibility! We certainly cannot claim to be perfect, but we do live as God's forgiven people, focused on following God's design for our lives. The more we study, guided by the Holy Spirit, the more accurately we see and understand that design.

Schooling

Homeschooling

When we look closely at the study, a lot more homeschooling goes on than we might have first thought. Those of us who've been blessed with the title "parent" have also received the additional title "teacher." Ephesians 6:4 challenges fathers to bring up their children in the training and instruction of the Lord. As part of the relationship with his child(ren), a father leads his family into a growing relationship with the heavenly Father.

Teachers need certain tools and attributes to be effective:

- The best teachers are also committed to being the best students. That brings us right back to the need for continual study at the feet of Rabbi Jesus.
- When they don't know the answers to their students' questions, good teachers say so and then search for the answers together with their students.
- A good teacher always shows up. Taking time to instruct may seem obvious, but it's easy for fathers/teachers to find excuses to play hooky from teaching.
- The best teachers have a deep love and respect for their students. If you don't respect your child as a dearly loved, chosen, and redeemed creation of God, how can you teach that child about God's great respect for him or her?

Homeschooling of this sort, raising our children in the Christian faith, is not optional for Christian parents. It's a calling from our Lord himself! And God didn't extend that calling only to parents. He extended it also to grandparents, to aunts and uncles, to friends and neighbors. The call goes out to all!

Homework

A Lesson Plan

Do you need some lesson-plan ideas for this week? Maybe these will get you started:

Monday   New Math with Peter—
                      The 70 x 7 Forgiveness Factor
                      Matthew 18:21–22

Tuesday   Home Economics with Mary and
                      Martha
                      Luke 10:38–42

Wednesday	Lunch Special—Five Loaves of Bread, Two Fish, and One Miracle *Matthew 14:13–21*
Thursday	Recess at the Jordan River *Mark 1:1–11*
Friday	Our Class Musical: "Singing with the Angels" *Luke 2:1–20*
Saturday	A Field Trip to Emmaus *Luke 24:13–35*
Sunday	Pep Rally for Team Members Who Are Running the Race *2 Timothy 4:7–8; Hebrews 12:1–2*

Sound like a good plan, a God-pleasing plan? I'll see you in the study! We may have thought the study went out of style along with Ward Cleaver, but leave it to Jesus—he knows what we need as we desire to live by God's design.

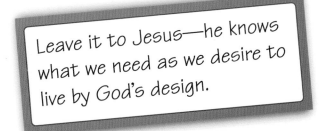

Leave it to Jesus—he knows what we need as we desire to live by God's design.

[Jesus said,] "Are you tired? Worn out? . . . Come to me. Get away with me and you'll recover your life.
I'll show you how to take a real rest. Walk with me and work with me—watch how I do it. Learn the unforced rhythms of grace. I won't lay anything heavy or ill-fitting on you. Keep company with me and you'll learn to live freely and lightly."

Matthew 11:28–30 THE MESSAGE

At day's end I'm ready for sound sleep, for you, God, have put my life back together.

Psalm 4:8 THE MESSAGE

Dear children, let us not love with words or tongue but with actions and in truth. This then is how we know that we belong to the truth, and how we set our hearts at rest in his presence whenever our hearts condemn us. For God is greater than our hearts, and he knows everything.

1 John 3:18–20 NIV

This is for the birds . . .

STEP #6
Cut out right roof
panel (fig. "f1") and left
roof panel (fig. "f2") as
indicated.

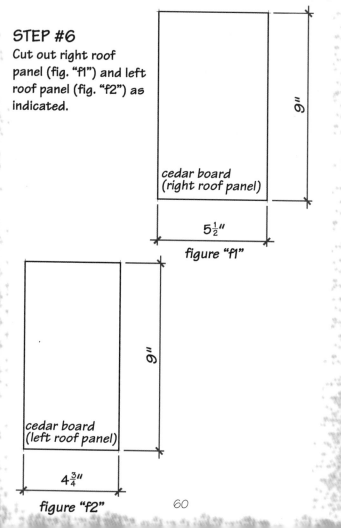

cedar board
(right roof panel)

9"

5½"

figure "f1"

cedar board
(left roof panel)

9"

4¾"

figure "f2"

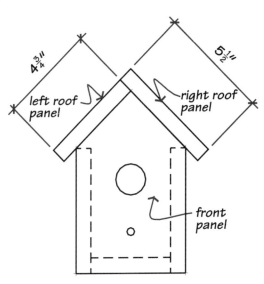

left roof panel

$4\frac{3}{4}''$

right roof panel

$5\frac{1}{2}''$

front panel

figure "g1"

FRONT ELEVATION

STEP #7

Install roof panels on birdhouse walls as shown in figures "g1" and "g2". Assemble roof panels with adhesive and nails (2 nails per end and 3 nails along ridge).

This is for us . . .

The Bedroom

"And now you know the rest of the story . . ."

Paul Harvey made that line famous. But God made it a reality. The Creator of the universe is into rest. He created it. He sanctified it. He designed us with a need for it.

For many, that's very refreshing news. Resting, napping, sleeping, and *guilt* often lie in the same bed. Before announcing, "Let's get rid of the guilt!" we need to note that God does not call us to laziness. In Proverbs, God's book of wisdom, at least sixteen passages speak against laziness. One of them, Proverbs 20:13, warns us:

> *Don't be too fond of sleep;*
> *you'll end up in the poorhouse.*
> *Wake up and get up;*
> *then there'll be food on the table.*
>
> THE MESSAGE

Even so, rest and sleep fall under the blanket of spiritual issues; namely, they're wonderful forms of prayer. Do you believe that? Stay with me now, and I will show you it's true!

When the apostle Paul wrote to the saints at Thessalonica (1 Thessalonians 5:17), he told them to pray continually. What used to disturb me was the difficulty of praying continually when we, as humans, sleep away so many hours of our lives.

A good night's sleep (or a
good day's nap) can be one
continual prayer to God.

Then, as though someone whacked me upside the head
with a pillow, it hit me. A good night's sleep (or a good
day's nap) can be one continual prayer to God.

Talk about beauty sleep! What a beautiful way to pray—
with your eyes closed! When we take care of our bodies by
getting enough sleep, we say to God, in effect, "I care about
this body you have entrusted to me. Thank you for this
opportunity to rest it. I honor you with this sleep." As our
bodies rest in sleep, our dreams and snores ascend to God as
prayers from his faithful stewards.

As humans, we require a certain amount of sleep to be able
fully to give God the glory he deserves when we're awake.
What a blessing to know that our heavenly Father hears all
our prayers, whether awake or asleep! His promise is that he
will not slumber or sleep. His ears are always attentive to
the prayers of his continually praying, faithful stewards.

So the next time you feel exhausted from work or play and
need a nap or a good night's sleep, tell your family, "I'm

going to the bedroom to take a prayer!" Then proceed to pray continually over the next several minutes or hours with your eyes closed!

Bedtime Prayer

The sixteenth-century reformer Martin Luther wrote a bedtime prayer to help Christians to live by God's design. It's a wonderful prayer, but I also love what he added just after the *Amen*. The prayer goes like this:

My Heavenly Father,
I thank You, through Jesus Christ, Your beloved
Son, that You have protected me, by Your grace.
Forgive, I pray, all my sins and the evil I have done.
Protect me, by Your grace, tonight. I put myself in your
care, body and soul and all that I have. Let Your holy
angels be with me, so that the evil enemy will not gain
power over me. Amen.

Trans. Robert E. Smith

Then go to sleep quickly and happily.

In a short prayer, we've said everything we need to say to make it possible for us to "go to sleep quickly and happily"!

- We've thanked God for his gracious protection through the day now past.
- We've reminded ourselves of the special relationship our heavenly Father has with us and we with him in the cross of his Son, Jesus.
- We've confessed our sins, knowing that in Jesus all of them have been washed away, forgiven.
- We've commended every aspect of our lives to him.
- We've asked God to send his angels to stand guard over us while we sleep, keeping Satan and his demons far from us.
- And we've expressed our confidence in our Lord's care, closing our prayer with the word *Amen,* meaning "So it will be!"

After all that, what could possibly keep us tossing and turning? We can quickly and happily go to sleep!

At Rest in Jesus

Isn't that what living by God's design is all about? Our Father knows us intimately, for he created us. He knows our need for physical rest. He also knows our need for spiritual rest and refreshment.

As we consider the bedroom of a life built upon the foundation of Jesus Christ, we realize that right from the

> Our Father knows us
> intimately, for he created us.

start he set apart a day of rest—the Sabbath, a time for
physical, spiritual, and family rest:

> *And on the seventh day God finished his work that he
> had done, and he rested on the seventh day from all his
> work that he had done. So God blessed the seventh day
> and made it holy, because on it God rested from all his
> work that he had done in creation.*
>
> Genesis 2:2–3

God did not create the human body to work seven days a
week. Instead, he brings his family together every Lord's
Day so we may find rest in him: rest in his forgiveness, his
protection, his promises, and his grace; rest in times of
fellowship with brothers and sisters in Christ; rest in the
study of his Word; rest in sharing the deepest longings and
prayers of our hearts; rest in singing his praise and giving
him thanks.

Truly, as we rest in Jesus and his gifts, we remember the *rest*
of his story.

Jesus rested physically and also found rest in prayer, in conversing with his Father:

> *And after [Jesus] had dismissed the crowds, he went up on the mountain by himself to pray. When evening came, he was there alone.*
>
> Matthew 14:23

> *Immediately Jesus made his disciples get into the boat and go on ahead of him to Bethsaida, while he dismissed the crowd. After leaving them, he went up on a mountainside to pray.*
>
> Mark 6:45–46 NIV

> *Then, because so many people were coming and going that they did not even have a chance to eat, he said to them, "Come with me by yourselves to a quiet place and get some rest."*
>
> Mark 6:31 NIV

Jesus knew about busy-ness, but he also knew about rest and its importance. He turned everything and everyone in his life over to his Father and rested, trusting his Father's blueprints for his life. What an example he left for us!

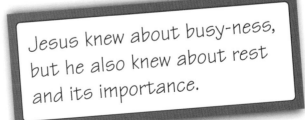

Jesus knew about busy-ness, but he also knew about rest and its importance.

A Reflection on Rest

Years ago I wrote the following reflection, which I'd like to share with you. When my children were young, God invited me into their rooms while they slept trustingly in his protective care. I often sat on each of their beds as their bodies rested. Returning to my computer one night, I wrote this:

It's nearing midnight. My children, you have been asleep for several hours now. These are some of my random bedside thoughts as your bodies and minds rest:

+ A few hours ago I prayed that the Lord and his angels would surround the three of you tonight. I wonder how many angels the Lord brought with him. Is the room angel-packed as I sit in their midst on this holy ground?

+ I wish I could put my ear to your head and listen to your dreams.

+ You are growing so very fast. I remember when we put you in your first big bed with the railing. This big bed doesn't look so big anymore, but you do!

+ I should have apologized for losing my patience with you today. You were just excited about doing something with me. You had spent the day in school and finally had a chance to run and shout. You have so much energy! I regret that I missed that time together. I will ask for your forgiveness tomorrow. I will ask God's forgiveness right now.

+ *Speaking of such energy, it's amazing to see your bodies so still after a day of running, talking, skipping rope, playing games, eating.*

+ *Now your bodies rest. You need it. God didn't create you with bionic bodies. I have much to learn from you. The day is for work (and play in your case), and the night is for sleeping.*

+ *When I tucked you in earlier, I said, "Sleep tight." I should have told you, "Sleep loose!" You'll have enough stress later in life that will cause sleep-tight nights. Sleep at peace.*

+ *Your rooms are filled with memories. As you grow older, I wonder what you will remember and what things you won't recall that your mom and I hoped you would.*

+ *Benjamin, I love the gift of your imagination in which you saw an entire secret fort in the mountains. You created it out of blankets and boxes for your brother and sister, but your mom and I enjoyed it just as much.*

+ *Sarah, thank you for the wonderful chalk pictures on the driveway that welcomed me home today. They were bright, creative, and fun. Tonight's rain will wash them away, but I'll keep a copy in my mental box of memories.*

+ *Christopher, that giggle spree you went on during supper when Daddy did something silly made my week. Thank you!*

+ *I love you—each of you—very, very much.*

Dear Guardian Sabbath Lord, Thank you for sending your angels to me—the ones I can't see and the ones named Benjamin, Sarah, and Christopher. Keep them marveling at your creation as they continue to teach me. Help me to love them as you love them. Amen.

Come, Rest

God's blueprint for our lives includes a room for rest, rest for our bodies and for our souls. With his divine hand the Son of God carved these words of invitation into the bedroom door:

Come with me by yourselves to a quiet place and get some rest.

Mark 6:31 NIV

How can you refuse that invitation?

Make a joyful noise
to the LORD,
all the earth!
Serve the LORD
with gladness!
Come into his presence
with singing! Know that
the LORD, he is God!
It is he who made us,
and we are his;
we are his people,
and the sheep
of his pasture.
Enter his gates
with thanksgiving,
and his courts with praise!
Give thanks to him;
bless his name!
For the LORD is good;
his steadfast love
endures forever,
and his faithfulness
to all generations.

Psalm 100

Rejoice in the Lord always.
I will say it again: Rejoice!
Let your gentleness
be evident to all.
The Lord is near.
Do not be anxious
about anything,
but in everything,
by prayer and petition,
with thanksgiving,
present your requests to God.
And the peace of God,
which transcends all
understanding,
will guard your hearts and
your minds
in Christ Jesus.

Philippians 4:4–7 NIV

And this is the testimony,
that God gave us eternal life,
and this life is in his Son.
Whoever has the Son has life;
whoever does not have the
Son of God does not have life.

1 John 5:11–12

This is for the birds . . .

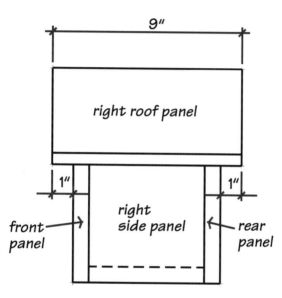

figure "g2"

SIDE ELEVATION

STEP #7 (cont.)

Install roof panels on birdhouse walls as shown in figures "g1" and "g2". Assemble roof panels with adhesive and nails (2 nails per end and 3 nails along ridge).

STEP #8

Cut a 4" long piece of 3/8" diameter wood dowel.
Glue and insert dowel into 3/8" dia. hole in front
panel as indicated.

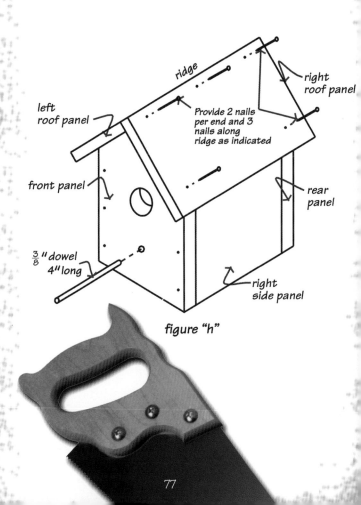

ridge

right
roof panel

left
roof panel

Provide 2 nails
per end and 3
nails along
ridge as indicated

front panel

rear
panel

$\frac{3}{8}$" dowel
4" long

right
side panel

figure "h"

This is for us . . .

The Living Room

L iving rooms are made for company. Maybe that's too broad a statement, but for the most part I think you'd agree. When company visits, we don't usually say, "Why don't we make ourselves comfortable in the kitchen . . . or in the bathroom . . . or in the study." When we keep company with others, the living room usually becomes our gathering place.

For this reason, it seems odd that the room has that title— *living* room. Depending on the traffic flow in your residence, you might find it difficult to say that a lot of *living* actually goes on there. You may not use your living room a lot; it may only rarely teem with actual living, with activity and joy.

Not enjoying the living room of our homes may not matter all that much. But I do pray that you enjoy the life, the abundant living, that Jesus died to win for you:

> *[Jesus said,] "I came that they may have life and have it abundantly."*
>
> John 10:10

I especially like the way Eugene Peterson translates that same verse in THE MESSAGE:

> *[Jesus said,] "I came so they can have real and eternal life, more and better life than they ever dreamed of."*

But what is God's living room like? Well, you've never seen a *living* room like this before! Our Lord isn't interested in a space marked off as the "living room" that in reality doesn't have much living going on in it. But Jesus is interested in each of us actually living real life!

Our God has built his *living* room on the foundation of Jesus Christ and Jesus' unconditional love. He in fact designed Christ's life and mission so we could live the abundant life he had in mind for us from all eternity. How do we go about living this abundant life by God's design?

First, we realize all of life is a gift from God. Then, daily as we head out into the world, we take these words of Paul with us and live by them:

> *Watch what God does, and then you do it, like children who learn proper behavior from their parents. Mostly what God does is love you. Keep company with him and learn a life of love. Observe how Christ loved us. His love was not cautious but extravagant. He didn't love in order to get something from us but to give everything of himself to us. Love like that.*
>
> Ephesians 5:1–2 THE MESSAGE

Here's the life plan again in bullet-point snippets:

- Watch how God lives, how Jesus lived while on earth.
- Keep company with him.
- Learn to live a life of love from him—not a life of selfishness from the world.
- Love extravagantly—don't hold back!
- Live and love, not because you're looking for something in return, but because Christ first loved you and gave his life for you.

Abundant Life—By Design

In other words, we live abundantly as we love abundantly in response to God's love for us. We model Jesus' life of love. The "living room" of our lives reflects God's own living room! And what an open, life-filled room it is! Let's take a look . . .

It seems to go on forever, so there's plenty of comfortable space here for everyone! Miraculously, Jesus keeps company with everyone who walks inside!

God has carpeted the floor with forgiveness, to cushion our falls. The walls are painted a miraculous shade of grace. Love seats abound in the room!

Hanging in the very center of the room is a lamp. From it streams light in the shape of the Savior's cross. That light never goes out.

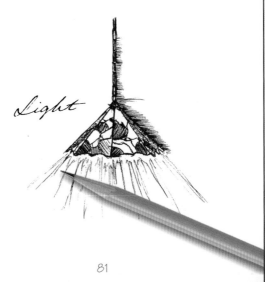

Light

Music of hope and praise bounces off the walls and into the ears of everyone in the living room.

The skylight offers us a glimpse of the heavenly life, eternal in God's presence, that will one day belong to all who know the Savior's pardon and peace here and now.

Pictures on the wall tell stories of those who in times past, with Jesus, once carried their own crosses and by his grace crucified their old desires. Those stories encourage all who live in Christ Jesus now.

As one of God's precious children, you have an open invitation to go on in, through the Door, Jesus Christ. You may make yourself at home there, leaving guilt, envy, lust, bitterness, gossip, worry, hatred, apathy, and all their friends at the doorstep. They aren't welcome.

As one of God's precious children, you have an open invitation to go on in, through the Door, Jesus Christ.

Go ahead! Walk on in through the Door, entering this room full of grace. Are you beginning to realize you've inherited a better life than you've ever dreamed possible?!

If so, enjoy yourself! Start living—truly living! That's the whole idea . . . it's *his* idea! It's God's plan for you as you live by his design.

The Door

Do not fear . . .
Do not let your hands
hang limp.
The LORD your God is with you,
he is mighty to save.
He will take great delight
in you, he will quiet you
with his love, he will rejoice
over you with singing.

Zephaniah 3:16–17 NIV

But let all who take refuge
in you rejoice; let them ever
sing for joy,
and spread your protection
over them, that those
who love your name
may exult in you.
For you bless the righteous,
O LORD;
you cover him with favor
as with a shield.

Psalm 5:11–12

He who dwells in the shelter
of the Most High
will rest in the shadow
of the Almighty.
I will say of the Lord,
"He is my refuge
and my fortress,
my God, in whom I trust."
Surely he will save you
from the fowler's snare
and from the deadly
pestilence.
He will cover you
with his feathers,
and under his wings you will
find refuge; his faithfulness
will be your shield and
rampart.

Psalm 91:1–4 NIV

This is for the birds . . .

Have you finished your birdhouse project yet? Or did you decide to postpone construction for another time?

Whether you've finished or not yet begun, you have no doubt noticed that the blueprints call for a foundation of sorts and a roof. That roof, though, covers only one room. The birds who make their home in it either already are or will soon become a close-knit family! Even so, their worries are few:

> *[Jesus said,] "Look at the birds of the air; they do not sow or reap or store away in barns, and yet your heavenly Father feeds them. Are you not much more valuable than they?"*
>
> Matthew 6:26 NIV

Yes, you are more valuable! You are the crown jewel of God's creation! He has welcomed you into his family. He has sent his own Son to die for you. He invites you to build your life upon the only sure foundation—the death and resurrection of Jesus Christ.

Now may your heavenly Father grant abundant blessings as you live out your life by his design—whether your physical house is a one-room studio apartment or a 120-room mansion!

This is for us . . .

The Roof

I had the oddest dream recently. I dreamt the roof blew off our house, but my family and I just tried to ignore it. We tried to continue living normally. Obviously, that wasn't going to happen!

My office had only the clouds in the sky as a roof. This caused me a lot of stress. On days when the sun lit up the sky, things weren't so bad—until, that is, a flock of geese flew over. They . . . how should I put it? . . . They must have mistaken my office for a bank because they left plenty of deposits!

At one point in my dream, dark skies rolled in, and it started to rain. I frantically tried to cover my computer, printer, and fax machine! My efforts proved completely useless. My books and office equipment were soon thoroughly soaked.

When the rain left, a cold front rolled in. I sat at my computer trying to type while wrapped in a warm coat and blankets. (I guess even in my dream I realized the futility of trying to type with winter mittens on! Maybe I'm smarter than I realized.) From that point on I don't remember any more of my dream. Maybe my brain froze!

The dream, odd as it seemed, helped me realize an important truth in a new way. I take so many of the blessings around me for granted. My dream reminded me that roofs serve quite an important purpose—every *shingle* one of them. (Sorry! That just slipped out!) I thanked God for the roof over my head when I woke up.

Roofless?

You can't live a normal life without a roof. First of all, think of all the protection it provides from outside elements—geese included! Without a roof to shut them out, birds, wild animals, and bugs would have free run in your entire house.

Second, a roof makes it possible to use every electrical appliance. A roof also keeps us from having to slather our faces daily with sunscreen. And it keeps those of us who live in the Midwest and North from having to shovel snow out of our houses day by day for several winter months!

All right . . . all kidding aside now. I hadn't thought about the blessings that come with a roof, but I can rest assured that God has.

And you can be assured that God's design for your spiritual life includes a good, sturdy roof, too. In fact, as you study his blueprint for your life, you'll learn that our Savior himself takes on the role. Jesus is not only our one sure foundation. He is also the protective roof above us.

He whispers in our ears, "Do not be afraid. I am your protection. I am your place of safety. You live under the shadow of my empowering cross." Like an eagle parent, Jesus covers you with his feathers, and under his wings you will find refuge (Psalm 91:4).

To benefit from his protecting love, though, we must give up our sinful, self-centered pride. And while we're at it, we might as well drop any self-serving and self-righteous attitudes.

Why? Because to benefit from Jesus' protecting care, we must first admit we need it! We confess our sins and admit our weaknesses. Yes, God invites us under his roof and into his family's home, but he asks that we submit our big heads to his bigger heart, so he can protect us fully, as only he can.

We leave our shoes at the door—for we enter to stand on holy ground. We enter to join in raising the roof with praise. Many of those praises center on our Lord's blueprints for our lives, the design for living we've been reading about in these pages:

- Through the work of the Holy Spirit, our Father has set us securely upon the immovable foundation of Jesus Christ.
- Guiding us through the family room, he has established our place in his family, the family that grows even closer day by day to our heavenly Father and to one another.
- He's given us perpetual access to his kitchen, where we can moment by moment taste and see his goodness toward us.
- He comes with us to the study, where he schools us in the promises of his Word, helping us to grow in our understanding of his design for our lives and in skills for living out that design.
- Jesus continually invites us to come away with him to learn how to take a real rest as we rest in him.
- Our Life-Giver has taken us to the living room, where he reveals to us the details of living out his abundant, meaning-filled life.
- Finally, he reminds us not to forget the importance of the roof, the promise of his protecting care, care in times of calm as well as storm.

Welcome to the living Stone,
the source of life.
The workmen took one look
and threw it out; God set it
in the place of honor. Present
yourselves as building stones
for the construction of a
sanctuary vibrant with life,
in which you'll serve as holy
priests offering Christ-
approved lives up to God.
The Scriptures provide
precedent:

Look! I'm setting a stone
in Zion, a cornerstone
in the place of honor.
Whoever trusts in this stone
as a foundation will never
have cause to regret it.

But you are the ones chosen
by God, chosen for the high
calling of priestly work,
chosen to be a holy people,
God's instruments to do his
work and speak out for him,
to tell others of the night-and-
day difference he made
for you—from nothing to
something, from rejected
to accepted.

1 Peter 2:4-6, 9-10 THE MESSAGE

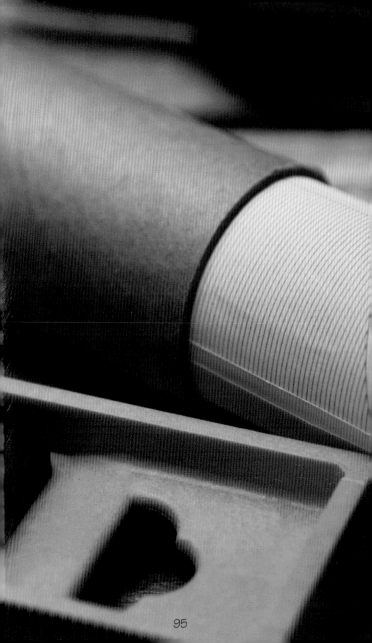

[Jesus said:]
"Everyone then who hears
these words of mine
and does them
will be like a wise man
who built his house on the rock.
And the rain fell,
and the floods came,
and the winds blew
and beat on that house,
but it did not fall,
because it had been founded
on the rock.
And everyone who hears
these words of mine
and does not do them
will be like a foolish man
who built his house on the sand.
And the rain fell,
and the floods came,
and the winds blew
and beat against that house,
and it fell,
and great was the fall of it."

Matthew 7:24-27